South Yorkshire Railway

on old picture postcards

Norman Ellis

1. Dunford Bridge station on the former Woodhead Great Central line between Penistone and Lancashire. Seen left to right are a water storage tank, sidings piled with flags, and the main station buildings. Stone quarrying was abundant in the area. Card published by Biltcliffe of Penistone, posted in 1908. Dunford was closed to passenger traffic in January 1970.

Printed by
Adlard Print and Typesetting Services,
Ruddington, Notts.

£3.50

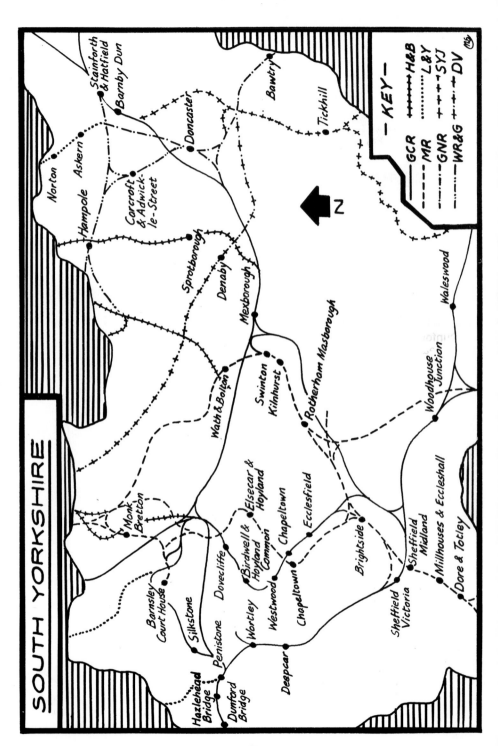

SOUTH YORKSHIRE

KEY

GCR ———— H&B
MR - - - - - L&Y
GNR ·········· SYJ
WR&G DV

Stainforth & Hatfield
Barnby Dun
Askern
Norton
Hampole
Doncaster
Corcroft & Adwick-le-Street
Sprotborough
Denaby
Mexborough
Bawtry
Tickhill
Waleswood
Woodhouse Junction
Rotherham Masborough
Wath & Bolton
Swinton
Kilnhurst
Monk Bretton
Dovecliffe
Elsecar & Hoyland
Birdwell & Hoyland Common
Chapeltown
Ecclesfield
Brightside
Sheffield Midland
Millhouses & Eccleshall
Dore & Totley
Sheffield Victoria
Barnsley Court House
Silkstone
Penistone
Wortley
Westwood
Chapeltown
Deepcar
Hazlehead Bridge
Dunford Bridge

N

2. Dunford Bridge station in LNER days. The train has just emerged from renowned Woodhead tunnel. The platform has gained a signal cabin to replace one which stood nearer the road bridge.

Contents

Other railways mentioned:
Manchester, Sheffield & Lincolnshire Railway (MS&L)
North Eastern Railway (NER)
London & North Eastern Railway (LNER)
London Midland & Scottish Railway (LMS)

The map opposite shows pre-grouping railway lines in South Yorkshire, plus stations which feature in the book. It is not to scale. Some less-important or mainly-freight lines have been omitted.

INTRODUCTION

In 1974, the Metropolitan County of South Yorkshire was created from part of the time-honoured West Riding. The new Metropolitan Districts of Sheffield, Rotherham, Doncaster and Barnsley were its constituents.

The specious carve-up separated the coal and steel based areas of the south from the textile based regions further north, which became West Yorkshire. In recent years, all these traditional industries have suffered from substantial decline. The complex rail networks in West and South Yorkshire had been born from a need to transport products and people.

Several railway companies became involved in South Yorkshire. The Great Central and Midland Railways exerted the greatest influence. Competition between these two companies resulted in duplication of stations as well as lines.

The Great Northern made Doncaster into a railway centre. The workaday Lancashire & Yorkshire had minimal influence, whilst the Hull & Barnsley was only moderately successful with its attempts to carry coal to Hull. The quirky Dearne Valley Railway was a brainchild of colliery companies. The West Riding & Grimsby was a joint venture which became vested in the Great Northern and Great Central.

Most railways were placed into four main groups in 1923, two of which directly affected South Yorkshire. These were the London & North Eastern and London, Midland & Scottish Railways.

Operational problems, which became apparent from about 1910 onwards, were escalated by the 1939-45 war. After the election of a Labour Government in 1945, the four groups were nationalised in 1947 to form British Railways. This was followed by phasing out of steam and implementation of the Beeching Plan which radically reduced the size of the country's rail network. In 1954, overhead electrification was completed on the former GCR line between Sheffield, Penistone and Manchester. This was a late example of rejuvenation.

For a time, many railway stations survived as tangible evidence of the great days of rail travel. Even where lines or stations were closed, the latter sometimes lived on as homes, industrial premises or overgrown ruins.

But the need for more unmanned stations, plus the necessity to reduce maintenance costs on buildings which became vandalised, led to replacement of many existing station buildings with bus-shelter type structures. Surviving large stations have not escaped some remodelling.

This book is a tribute, almost a memorial, to the many vanished or transformed railway stations in South Yorkshire. All the pictures are reproduced from photographic type postcards in the author's collection. Most of them were issued during the first two decades of the twentieth century. They show a unique and varied type of Victorian, occasionally Edwardian, architecture which has largely disappeared.

Norman Ellis
July 1994

ISBN 0 946245 88 6

Designed and Published by
Reflections of a Bygone Age,
Keyworth, Nottingham

3. Sturdy, stone station buildings at **Hazlehead Bridge,** between Dunford Bridge and Penistone. The station served a scattered community. The lean-to portion was new when the photo was taken. A minor branch led from the station to Hepworth Iron Company's works at Crow Edge, which provided local work.

4. The lean-to building (mentioned earlier) on the end of **Hazlehead Bridge** station house replaced a structure destroyed in the accident pictured above. Both these cards were produced by Biltcliffe of Penistone. The station itself closed to passenger traffic in March 1950 and to goods trains in May 1964.

Station Architecture

Most railway stations incorporated certain basic features. Stations built by a particular railway company, especially if they stood on the same line, were often architecturally similar. Beyond these criteria, railway station design was characterised by individuality.

Form and size depended on location, potential business, availability of building materials, the company's financial state, the architect's fancy, even a local landowner's whim.

Village railway stations usually had a booking hall, waiting rooms (with coal fires), toilets, possibly a stationmaster's house and a goods office. Sometimes, all these features were housed in a building on one platform. The opposite side of this building usually faced the approach road. The other platform may only have possessed a passenger shelter. Platforms were commonly connected by a footbridge or subway.

Where there was a road bridge above the station, the main station building was frequently placed adjacent to it, the platforms then having little more than waiting accommodation. Alongside a lot of village or township stations were goods sidings.

Large city or town stations had all the features of country stations, sometimes repeated on several platforms. Refreshment rooms, bookstalls and administrative offices were additional features. A concourse or an overall roof, if incorporated, added a touch of luxury.

Railway stations in South Yorkshire had to cater for an area which was part industrial and part agricultural. They were, on the whole, functional without being remarkable. Notable exceptions existed at each end of the scale.

The Dearne Valley Railway used old rail coaches as waiting rooms. The facade of Barnsley Court House station was second-hand. The Midland Railway probably was not seen at its best in the region.

The Manchester, Sheffield & Lincolnshire Railway, which became the Great Central in 1897, developed its own pleasing style of station in the 1860s, which later manifested itself at Chapeltown, Deepcar, Mexborough, Silkstone and Woodhouse, all illustrated herein. The design comprised two gabled end buildings joined by a central block with verandah roof on columns. The configuration had umpteen variations and appeared outside South Yorkshire.

Several stations on the West Riding & Grimsby Railway had what may be described as an attractive chapel-cum-cottage style, Carcroft, illustrated later, being a good example. Some of these stations were in West Yorkshire.

Front cover: **Penistone** station when it was a significant railway centre *(see also illustrations 6 & 7).*
Back cover (top): **Carcroft & Adwick-le-Street** on the WR & G line between Doncaster and Wakefield. *(see also illustrations 43 and 44).*
　　　　　(bottom): **Ecclesfield** Great Central on a card by J. Crowther Cox of Rotherham. *(see also illustration 15).*

5. Silkstone station, east of Penistone, was erected about 1877 and is pictured around three decades later. The main station building demonstrates a typical MS&L design, with twin pavilions joined by a central block. The single track behind the water column led to a cattle loading dock. The postcard, in the 'Haigh' series, was sent from Barnsley in November 1906. Passenger trains ceased in June 1959, and goods traffic nearly four years later.

6. In 1874, the original **Penistone** station was resited, as above, slightly further east. The station witnessed much freight and passenger activity. Colliery owned wagons and part of Cammell Laird's huge steelworks, which were closed and demolished in the early 1930s, are visible.

7. Penistone was an important railway crossroads, with lines to Huddersfield, Barnsley, Sheffield and Manchester. This and the previous view, by Biltcliffe of Penistone, show opposite ends of the main part of the station, looking east, around 1910. Today, Penistone station is vastly diminished in size and status.

DENISTONE STATION

8. Wortley station, looking towards Penistone. It served Wortley village, which was largely rebuilt last century by the first Lord Wharncliffe. Although set in farming country, iron forges existed nearby. The Biltcliffe card shows many interesting station features. Wortley was on the main line, but lost its stopping passenger trains in May 1955.

9. The main station building at **Deepcar** (for Stocksbridge) was of the familiar MS&L twin-pavilion type, left. The deep valance on one of the opposite structures, right, gave added weather protection. Samuel Fox's railway branched from Deepcar to serve his steelworks at Stocksbridge. The last passenger train stopped in June 1959. Postcard published by Bradbury of Deepcar.

10. In 1851, **Sheffield Victoria** station was opened on the north side of the city by the MS&L (later Great Central). On this card, posted in 1908, the distant station is flanked by the Royal Victoria Hotel, left, which was opened by Sheffield Hotel Company in 1862 and absorbed by the MS&L in 1883. The end came for this important station in January 1970.

11. Much timber went into construction of the station at **Waleswood**, near the Derbyshire border. For obvious reasons, chimneys were brick. If well-maintained, wooden station buildings lasted surprisingly well. Card by Bramwell & Son, Sheffield. The station closed in March 1955.

12. Relatively isolated, but within sight of pit heaps, **Dovecliffe** station, as befits its name, had a rustic appearance, with gardens and wall creeper. Eight lamps are discernible. At extreme right is the signal box, three storeys high. Card posted from Barnsley in 1904. *"I think you will know this view!"* Dovecliffe closed in December 1953.

13. The exact location of **Birdwell & Hoyland Common** station was dictated by Lord Wharncliffe, who insisted it be near his new colliery. The medley of buildings in this c.1905 view, although not architecturally inspiring, look ample and tidy. Ten trains a day stopped here in each direction in 1910, as at next-door Dovecliffe, and passenger trains similarly ceased in 1953.

14. The second **Westwood** station, built in 1876, shown here c.1906, was distant from any large settlement. The elevated signal cabin controlled sidings and the gated crossing. The other platform was behind the photographer. Stationmaster and family are outside the station house. Total closure came early, in October 1940.

15. Ecclesfield Great Central, partly shown here c.1906, cost £1985 to built in 1876, including approach road and sidings. Observe the decorative bargeboarding on the station house. The other platform was on the left, beyond the footbridge. This station almost rubbed shoulders with the Midland counterpart. It closed in 1953.

16. Posed but splendid view of **Chapeltown** Great Central. The staggered platforms each have substantial buildings. Beyond the farthest structure, left, a spur ran north to the ironworks complex. The nine uniformed railway servants are in contrast to today's unstaffed stations. Goods traffic survived for 16 months after the passenger service ceased in December 1953.

17. Woodhouse Junction station, with good representation of the MS&L design which was based upon twin gabled pavilions and a joining central block with verandah. Here, the farthest section was the stationmaster's house. The opposite platform had a similar smaller conformation. Card posted from Sheffield in 1904.

GREAT CENTRAL STATION, MEXBRO.

18. At **Mexborough,** the basic MS&L design of twin pavilions plus connecting block reached a degree of flamboyance, with appendages to gable ends, elaborate bay windows, and a cavernous-looking central alcove behind twin arches. Mexborough station was resited to the location shown in 1871.

19. The buildings at **Mexborough,** seen here from the opposite end, were fine and functional. The two views combine to show interesting station paraphernalia, such as barrows, fire buckets, vending machines, weighing scales, a clock and the inevitable adverts.

20. Set in farming country, **Barnby Dun** station looked decidedly rural. The delightful main building faced an innovative ramp. Observe the two milk churns. The card was posted from the village in 1908; in 1913, with line widening between Doncaster and Thorne, Barnby Dun station was rebuilt. Closure came in September 1967.

21. When the GCR line between Doncaster and Thorne was widened, **Stainforth & Hatfield** station (as it was usually called) was rebuilt. The extensive layout is shown here in post-grouping days, probably c.1930. The colliery is Hatfield Main.

22. Small **Monk Bretton** station was characteristically country Midland in design. It closed as early as 1937. Monk Bretton village, a good mile east of Barnsley, became famous for its priory and, to a lesser degree, its colliery.

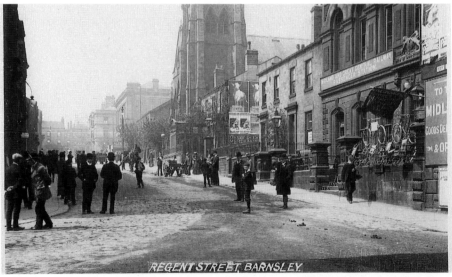

23. Barnsley Court House station was opened in 1870, because of cramped conditions at Barnsley Exchange Station, which had opened in 1850. The MR, which was largely responsible for its construction, purchased the former Court House building for use as ticket office. This is shown, right, on a card by Thomas Lamb of Barnsley which was sent to Ulverston in June 1926. Passenger trains to Barnsley Court House ceased in April 1960.

24. Barnsley Court House station was used by the Mid[...]
postcards and several now-defunct magazines and ne[...]
appears on the lamp.

I.W.BURKINSHAW & Cº
Artificial Teeth
PAINLESS EXTRACTIONS
1&3, BECKETT Sᵗ Barnsley

POTTS&SONS

GET IT AT
BARNSLEY BRITISH
DRAPERY STORES

NS, LTᴰ. LONDON, E.C.

GRAPHIC
THE WAR
AEROPLANING
MANY PHASES

d Great Central Railways. Included on its bookstall were
rs. Observe the boy with the basket. The town name

25. For stations on its direct Barnsley to Sheffield line, the Midland favoured simple platform shelters. These were complemented by a larger peripheral building with booking facilities. The arrangement is highlighted at **Chapeltown** above. The larger structure is visible immediately left of the bridge. Card by N.T. Furniss, Sheffield, posted to Huddersfield in April 1918.

26. The same **Chapeltown** station in LMS days. Each waiting shelter had a first class and a general waiting room. The square buildings near fire buckets housed gentlemen's toilets. The signal box beyond the bridge controlled goods sidings to the right of the station. Card published by Marshall of Chapeltown.

27. Elsecar & Hoyland, a Midland station on the same line as Chapeltown. Note the similarities, also differences, in layout. Goods sidings existed to the right. At left is a water tank and, nearer bridge, a water crane. Card by E.L Scrivens, Doncaster, sent to York in July 1912.

28. Elsecar & Hoyland (name is on the gaslamps) in LMS days, when it was fashionable and possible to hire a train for a day trip.

29. This view at **Brightside,** near Sheffield, shows that MR gable ended waiting shelters were supplemented by canopied ones. Notice the unusual chimneys, including those on the booking office building beyond the wall. Similar chimneys existed at Chapeltown and Elsecar.

30. Busy scene at **Kilnhurst,** where an island and side platforms had small amiable waiting rooms plus plenty of gaslamps. The poster, strategically sited at the end of an approach, was for tourist tickets to England, Scotland, Wales and Ireland. Kilnhurst West closed in January 1968.

31. Attractive but not over-finicky building, advantaged by lofty chimney stacks, which formed the exterior of **Swinton** station. Various signs indicate the booking office, waiting room, cloakroom, parcels office, telegraph office and stationmaster's room. Card published by C.F. Hurst, stationer, Swinton, posted in 1905. Station closure came in January 1968.

32. When the North Midland Railway completed a line from London to Leeds, Sheffield was bypassed. Rectification came in 1870 when its successor, the Midland Railway, established a line along the Sheaf Valley and opened **Sheffield Midland** station. Its W.H. Smith bookstall is shown.

33. For its size, Wath-upon-Dearne was well favoured with three stations – Great Central, Midland and Hull & Barnsley – all reached from appropriately named Station Road. The above simple timber waiting rooms formed part of the Midland offering, actually called **Wath & Bolton** because of its location between the two places.

ROTHERHAM (MASBOROUGH STATION.)

34. Rotherham and its environs were served by lines and stations of the MR and GCR. **Rotherham Masborough,** a Midland property, had island and side platforms. This typical W.H. Smith postcard would have been on sale at their bookstall, visible on the platform. The card was posted at Rotherham in September 1917.

MASBRO STATION.
S. W. & S.

35. Rotherham Masborough station experienced several name changes. It opened in 1840 as Masborough, became Masborough & Rotherham in 1896, Rotherham Masborough in 1908 and Rotherham in 1969. Card by S. Wilson & Son, Rotherham, posted from the town in 1904. *"How do you like this view of our station. Does it look like a village one?"* wrote Beatty.

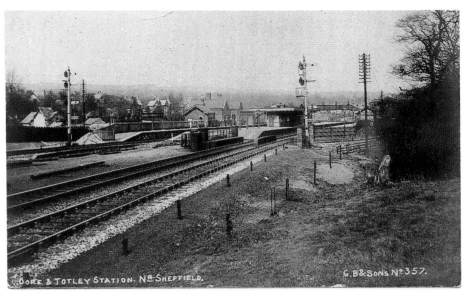

36. Following an increase in traffic, the Midland line from Dore northwards was quadrupled in 1901-3. **Dore & Totley** station took the form shown here, looking north. The main building on the west side remained, but the other buildings and platforms illustrated, including the island, were elements of the widening.

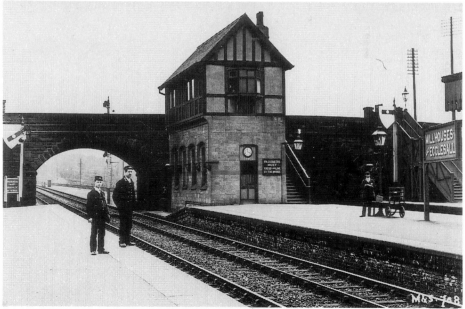

37. Millhouses & Eccleshall station also was widened in 1901-3. It acquired an island platform which was reached from a bridge via the tall stone/timber building and staircase illustrated. Card by Morgan & Sons, Sheffield.

38. Unlike Barnsley, Rotherham & Sheffield, **Doncaster** had only one station. An important interchange for freight and human cargo, it became particularly busy on St. Leger days. The Great Northern line to King's Cross was opened during 1849-52, from which time Doncaster station on the above site dates.

ASTER,

No 102. RAILWAY STATION. DONCASTER.

39. Interior of **Doncaster** station, looking north, contemporary with previous view, early 1900s. The footbridge led to the famous locomotive, carriage and wagon works, left, which were established in 1853.

455. Railway Station. Bawtry J.S.&S.

40. The individual style of the principal station building at **Bawtry** was carried through to the chimney columns. The small town of Bawtry, marginally within Yorkshire, was served by the GNR main line to the south. Card published by J. Simonton & Sons of Balby.

BAWTRY STATION 226. —WELCHMAN RETFORD.

41. As befitted a busy line, the platforms at **Bawtry** were long and white-edged; any monotony was relieved by flower beds. The small timber shelters were characteristically Great Northern, but the ecclesiastical arches, visible at left, were a bonus.

F LS 53-44. Sprotborough Station.

42. The Hull & Barnsley Railway was constructed to convey Yorkshire coal to Hull and break the North Eastern Railway monopoly there. Towards its western extremity, the H&B line diverged at Wrangbrook. One prong had **Sprotborough** station, opened in 1894, later recorded by Scrivens, above. From 1903, the station handled freight only, until it closed in August 1964.

E.L.S. 18-20. RAILWAY STATION, CARCROFT &

43. The line between Doncaster and Wakefield now forms part of the trunk route from London to Leeds. It originated as the independent West Riding & Grimsby (absorbed by the GCR/GNR in 1897). Four of the stations were generally to the design captured here at **Carcroft & Adwick-le-Street** by E.L. Scrivens of Doncaster. Goods traffic ended here in June 1965, passenger trains two years later.

44. Exterior of **Carcroft & Adwick-le-Street** station. The ostentatious design of the main building, here in rock faced stone, with hipped roofs and a spire, was curious for a colliery area. The signal box was more conventional.

45. In contrast and decidedly basic, **Hampole** was another station on the WR&G. The line-up includes two railway staff. A station house existed: this card was posted to it from Leeds on 5th August 1905 by the stationmaster's daughter, who'd just travelled into the city. Hampole station survived until January 1952.

46. The Wakefield, Pontefract & Goole Railway (which became part of the Lancashire & Yorkshire Railway) had a rural branch from Knottingley to Doncaster via Norton and Askern. Its stations at Womersley and Norton possessed a Swiss-cottage look, evident at **Norton,** above. Card posted from Askern in 1907.

47. Askern station and its approach had a positive air of respectability when this photo was taken, probably around 1907. Askern's potential as a spa town was overshadowed by the coming of its colliery in 1911. Both these stations closed to passengers in March 1947 and goods traffic in October 1964.

48. Few new stations were opened to passenger traffic after 1902, but an exception was the South Yorkshire Joint Railway which was opened for minerals in January 1909 and to passengers in December 1910. It was used by the GCR, GNR, L&Y, MR and NER. Here, one of the stations, **Tickhill,** is under construction, probably in 1907. Note the temporary tracks.

49. Later stage of construction at **Tickhill,** captured from a similar spot. Station buildings look almost complete; two workmen, right, have an unenviable roadmaking task. Coal was the incentive for constructing this belated railway, which ran from Kirk Sandall to Dinnington, via Maltby and Tickhill, later called Tickhill and Wadworth.